Girl, You Can Do Anything

Ignite Your Inner Strength Through Inspiring Stories of Courage, Confidence, Determination, and Friendship

Hayden Fox

Table of Contents

The Lands of Whimsy and Wisdom (The Author's Note)

Magical creatures have spread across the world. They live in fields and forests, palaces and tree houses—even in the clouds. At first, it might seem like different magical creatures aren't too much like one another, but each of them is special in their own way. They are compassionate and thoughtful. They are adventurous and independent. They are brave and honest. They will speak up when they need help or when they see that others need it. They may make mistakes, but each and every one of them is trying the best they can.

By trusting themselves, discovering what makes them unique, and working together, they may discover they can create things far greater than they could ever accomplish on their own. By listening and understanding, they can discover that, perhaps, they have more in common than they ever realized.

When you read these stories, I hope you will find what makes you unique as well, and see that you—and the people you know—are all growing into something really special.

A Magical Cast of Characters

Wist Willowflower: A curious girl who loves to explore and try new things.

Beauty, Soul of the Forest: A great and ancient tree that helps the things around it grow. Keeps itself hidden most of the time, but might make an exception for the right person.

Sherry the Mouse: A tiny mouse determined to keep a tidy and cheerful home, no matter what it takes.

Brim the Lava Lizard: Lives alone underground. Likes it that way. Really, he just wants to get comfortable and stay very, very warm.

Curio: A helpful but lonely cockatrice who just wants to find her place in the world.

The King's Messenger: A hardworking servant who, honestly, has way too many things to do.

Princess Persephone: A mysterious princess who would rather be left alone.

Kiria, Queen of Artasia: The queen of the kingdom in the sky. She controls the weather, the sun, the moon, and the stars, and makes sure everyone below is taken care of.

Cora, Nadia, Ravea, and Shine: The daughters of Queen Kiria, each capable and resourceful in their own way.

Pinn the Quiet Goblin: A goblin who would rather read and play quietly than be noisy and run around. It's hard for her to think when there's too much going on!

Goblins: It's a well-known fact that goblins sure do love to have fun. A goblin can do pretty much anything if they set their mind to it, but they generally aren't very quiet about it.

Molly the Minotaur: A big and bulky monster who loves flowers, nature, and sunshine more than anything.

Garonar the Minotaur: A much more traditional monster who loves musty cave walls, dark passageways, and everything strong and spooky.

Terrin the Gnome: A delightfully cheerful neighbor of Molly's. If there was an apple cobbler baking contest, she would win it for sure.

The Offer of the Deep Forest

Wist Willowflower looked out the window of the small, one-room building where she went to school each day. It was beautiful outside. The trees were huge and green, the birds sang loudly, and soft, white clouds hung in the light-blue sky. There was a whole world to explore, and Wist couldn't wait.

Her teacher, a tall elf with long, pointed ears and a tight bun in her yellow hair, tapped the blackboard pointedly. "Miss Wist, it's important to pay attention, even on the last day of school."

I am paying attention, Wist thought. *I'm just paying attention to the outdoors.* But she understood what her teacher meant, and she tried her very best to pay attention to the lesson. Under the desk, she gently kicked the picnic basket she had brought to school. Wist had asked her mother if she could go exploring when school was over, and her mother, ever encouraging, had packed her some snacks for the afternoon.

The school day felt like it lasted forever. The outdoors and all its wonderful mysteries called to Wist. She never knew what she might find. A busy beehive? A beaver building a dam in a river? A mysterious sword waiting to be discovered? Wist had no idea, and that was part of the fun.

After a long day of patiently waiting, her teacher dismissed the class and wished them a good summer. Wist was determined to make the most of it, starting today.

She left through the fields, touching the top of the tall grass with the tips of her fingers and feeling the warmth of the sun on her face. She bubbled with excitement, but resisted the urge to hurry. She wanted to enjoy where she was just as much as she enjoyed thinking about where she could go.

The forest called to her. She had explored it many times before, and it was one of her favorite places. It was full of life, with buzzing and birdsong and creatures rustling along the forest floor or high in the trees. Wist walked quietly and carefully when she was in the forest, and she was rewarded when animals let her get close and watch them. Sometimes, she liked to imagine she was part of the forest itself.

Today, she went further into the forest than she ever had before. At first, the trees were far apart. Wist could still see the beautiful blue sky above her. But as she traveled, the trees became larger and grew closer together, creating such a thick canopy that when she looked up, Wist saw only green leaves. The shadows were long and deep.

She even found a fairy mushroom circle, which she was careful not to disturb. The forest felt more mysterious than ever, although not dangerous as long as she was cautious.

It became difficult to travel, with roots from the great trees blocking her way. Sometimes she would find a path, but more and more she had to make her own. Wist imagined she could see trees moving in the distance. But that had to be her imagination… right?

A gust of wind blew through the leaves, and Wist thought she heard a faint whisper. "Who walks among my brothers and sisters?" it asked. At least, she thought so. It was very hard to hear.

Wist stood as still as she could. She knew it just had to be the wind. But she wanted to hear it again, so she tried her hardest to make no sound at all. There was another gust of wind, and Wist heard again, "Who walks among my brothers and sisters?" It was still very quiet, but clearer this time.

It felt uncomfortable to break the silence with her voice, like the feeling of talking too loudly inside a library. But if she had been asked a question, shouldn't she answer it?

"My name is Wist Willowflower, and I mean no harm," she said. "I love this place more than any other, and so I came to visit." Wist waited patiently. If she was being honest, she was beginning to feel silly, talking to herself in the woods.

The wind blew through the leaves again, and the voice was clear now. "Come this way, if you wish."

A strange thing happened then. Wist didn't see any of the trees or leaves move at all, but slowly, a path became clear—the dirt smooth and easy to travel over, the leaves from the trees forming a welcoming arch. She was certain nothing had moved, and certain the path wasn't there before. But there it was, and the more she thought about it, the less certain she was. She decided she would find no answers by staying put, and she had set out to explore that day, so explore she would.

Wist walked down the path. Sometimes, she would look back expecting to see that the path had disappeared, but it remained behind her, clear and safe. She thought maybe she was being watched, but she still felt no danger. Perhaps it was her imagination, but the sunny day, clear path, and thick canopy made her feel safe and protected.

She wondered where the path was taking her. The trees around her became so large and thick that she would have struggled to squeeze between them to leave the path, and she was a child. An adult most certainly would not fit. She had the feeling that the path was clear for her, but it could just as easily have turned into a great maze for someone unwelcome. Wist still walked slowly and carefully until the trail came to an abrupt end.

A great tree blocked her way entirely. It was far larger than any tree she had ever seen. It might be bigger than any tree *anyone* had ever seen. The trunk was a deep brown and so wide, it was nearly as large as her schoolhouse. The leaves were huge and green, but small, transparent rainbows shone onto the forest floor from the sunlight above.

"Do not be scared," a soothing voice said.

Wist couldn't imagine being scared here. This was the most peaceful place she had ever been.

"Thank you," Wist said. "I'm not." She was always respectful of nature and saw no reason to change now that part of it was speaking to her.

"It has been many, many seasons since I have met one of your kind," the voice said. "A person who stops to listen and acts with care is a rare person indeed."

This surprised Wist, because she knew plenty of other people who cared about others and who liked paying close attention to things—although perhaps they cared in different ways or paid attention to different things. She had a friend at school who loved math, another who loved astronomy, and another who loved to sing. She even had friends who cared about something different every week. And they all cared for each other very much in their own way, like her friend who loved to give advice, which was a way of caring about something and caring about others at the same time.

Still, Wist felt like it was a good time to listen and share, not start an argument. "Thank you," she said a second time. "It is a pleasure to meet you. I know a lot of people, and most of them are lovely."

"Hmm," the voice said. It was the same sort of sound Wist's mother made when she didn't necessarily agree, but didn't want to discourage her daughter, either.

"May I sit with you?" Wist asked. "I've walked quite a long way today."

"You may," the tree offered.

Wist sat under the tree, leaning comfortably against it. It was welcoming and warm. It made her sleepy. "Is there a name I should call you?"

"I rarely need a name. You can call me what you like," the voice said.

Wist thought for a moment. "I will call you Beauty, if you think that's a good name." She had a friend who had named her horse Beauty, and another friend who had named her turtle the same thing. It was perhaps unoriginal, but it was still, well, beautiful.

The sun was warm and the forest was comforting. She was safe and in good company. It was the perfect first day of summer. The unlikely pair didn't speak for a while. They simply enjoyed being together. Wist drifted off to sleep.

When she woke, she was surprised to see flowers surrounding her on all sides. She was at the center of a sweet-smelling rainbow, with flowers of yellow, orange, pink, red, and even some vibrant blues and purples. It was the most amazing thing she had ever seen in her whole life, and it had sprung up in the time it took to take a nap.

"Do you like the gift I have grown for you?" the great tree asked.

"I love it," Wist said. "Truly."

"You are welcome to stay here as long as you like," Beauty offered. "I would like you to stay here forever. I would provide you with everything, and ask you for nothing. Your roots could grow here, as deep and strong as my own."

At first, Wist wanted to point out that she had legs, not roots. However, she decided Beauty already knew that and must be speaking in metaphor, which is what adults called it when they said one thing but meant another.

Wist thought about the offer. She had found the perfect place. She couldn't imagine anywhere better, or any being more kind. She could live here the rest of her days, and she would be happy.

"I'm sorry," Wist apologized. "It's a wonderful offer, but I can't stay."

"Oh?" Beauty sounded surprised and disappointed.

Wist stretched and let out a yawn, still waking up. "This may be the most beautiful, magical, safe place I ever find. But I won't know unless I go and look, will I? I'd like to go on an adventure. Not just one, but lots of them, of all different kinds. Maybe when I'm old, I could come back and share the stories of all my journeys."

Wist knew, even as a small girl, that there was nothing wrong with being comfortable. On the other hand, she also didn't want to become so comfortable that she forgot to learn and explore. She knew that there would be times she would miss this place very much. But every time her mother packed her a lunch and sent her off to explore, she would remind Wist that the best thing about home was that you could always return.

Wist was still very young. She had so much time to decide who she was going to be and how she was going to use her energy. She could sail the seas, climb the mountains, sit and study, or map the stars. She could live alone or in a bustling city, far from her mother or right next door. She could make friends or even find love—or not, as she chose. She would be the one to decide where she was going, and she would change her mind whenever it made her happy.

It was scary for her to walk away from such a beautiful place, but if she had found this place, how many other wonders must there be? There was a world of adventure out there for her to see, and she wanted to see it all.

A branch from the tree bent down to Wist. To her surprise, it fell off, landing gently next to her. Beauty said softly, "A walking stick for all your adventures. As long as you hold it, it can take you back to this place. You are forever welcome."

Wist knew it was true, and for the rest of her life, the walking stick would be one of her greatest treasures.

The Mouse and the Monster

Sherry the Mouse liked to keep things tidy. Her house was tidy, her garden was tidy, and even the dirt path leading from her tiny garden to her tiny house was tidy.

Until recently.

For the last month, everything around her... rumbled. It wasn't an earthquake, exactly, or if it was, it was a tiny one. But it gave her tidy house and tidy garden just enough of a shake that she had to clean up again. Then, she would have to go out to the garden and pick up any of the carefully made signs that had fallen over. Sherry already spent a lot of time keeping things in order, but now it was just too much.

"These earthshakes are unacceptable," Sherry said with a frown, cleaning up a broken dish for the second time in a week. "And it feels like it's getting warmer in here every time it happens, too."

Sherry preferred to live by herself, but that meant that she needed to be extra resourceful. If there was something that needed done, she had to do it herself. And she wasn't exactly sure what needed to be done about these earthshakes, but *something* certainly did.

She started by exploring around her house and yard, but she didn't have much luck. All she discovered were more chores that needed doing. She widened her search, going out into the fields around her house, past her wooden fence, and into the tall grass. Sherry didn't get very far before she spotted a small wisp of smoke winding its way into the air. It was time to investigate!

She wasn't sure what to expect. Maybe a friend or a new neighbor? Sometimes when it was cold, Sherry liked to use her fireplace. The crackling fire kept her warm as plumes of smoke cheerily puffed out her chimney. But, it was summer now, and she hadn't used her own fireplace in months.

When Sherry got closer, she discovered the source of the smoke wasn't a house at all. It was coming from a long, jagged crack in the ground. She tried to peer in for a better look, but it was too dark and smoky.

"Well, that's not ideal," Sherry mumbled.

However, it was going to take more than a little smoke and a dark hole to stop her from solving the problem. She fished through her backpack and pulled out a large pair of goggles to protect her eyes, a handkerchief to wrap over her nose and mouth, and a small lantern to light the way. She double-checked her pack to ensure she had all the snacks and water she might need and that everything was fastened securely, then hopped down into the hole.

Sherry slid a short way, covering herself in dust, before finding her footing. Smoke clung to the rocky ceiling, but the lamp cast just enough light for her to see. Sherry checked behind her to make sure she would be able to climb out, and then she continued on.

The journey was decidedly unwelcoming. The floor was uneven, with pebbles that surprised her and made her stumble. Sometimes the path was wide, while other times it was so small she had to squeeze through, scraping an elbow or tearing part of her outfit. Other cracks lined the walls, some big enough that she could have turned down them if she wanted to. Whenever she found a path where she could turn, she marked her way by tying a piece of red ribbon to a rock so she could find her way home. Then, she would look to see which way the smoke was flowing and walk toward the source.

Sherry had the sense she was moving downward, but it was hard to tell how far she had traveled. Everything looked the same—until it didn't. A faint glow seemed to be coming from up ahead, although Sherry couldn't see its source.

The path turned again, sloped downward, and then abruptly ended. Sherry stood on the edge of a steep cliff and had an amazing view of a huge, underground cavern. There were jagged rocks sticking up from the floor, and the ceiling was so high that it was shrouded in darkness. At the bottom, there was an orange, glowing pool of lava.

"Well, that's going to be a problem," Sherry said.

Then, as she watched, a massive lizard crawled from a dark corner and flopped right into the lava, splashing it in every direction. When it did, the cavern shook and rumbled. Dust and rocks fell to the floor and into the lava pit.

"At least I solved the earthshake mystery," Sherry observed. "Although I'm not really sure what to do about it."

But just because Sherry didn't know what to do didn't mean she was ready to give up. She watched the lizard splashing and thrashing in the lava, like it was trying to get comfortable. It made such a commotion Sherry was worried the path might cave in behind her, but at least the lizard was so big and she was so small that she didn't have to worry about being spotted.

Eventually, the lizard found just the right spot and fell asleep. It snored loudly, filling the cavern with a low rumble. Sherry noticed that the lizard didn't have sharp teeth or ferocious claws and looked more content and peaceful than anything else—or, at any rate, how Sherry imagined a peaceful and content lava lizard would look.

"I wonder what he eats down here," Sherry said to herself. "Although, I think that's the lizard's problem. I have enough problems of my own right now." At the very least, the creature looked far too big to enjoy eating a mouse, which was good enough for Sherry.

She climbed down the side of the cliff, hanging a piece of ribbon from the top so she would know which of the many cracks in the wall would lead her home. It was an easy climb for her. With so many jagged and uneven pieces, she had plenty of handholds to grab and even crevices to stop and rest when she needed to.

When Sherry got to the bottom, she was careful to stay far away from the lizard. It didn't look like it meant her any harm, but if the lizard rolled over in its sleep and squished her or splashed her with lava, she would be in for a very bad day indeed. She wasn't sure if it would be a good idea to wake it up, and she didn't know how she would do that anyway, so she helped herself to a small picnic out of her backpack while she waited.

Long after her meal was finished, the lizard woke up, and rolled over in the lava with a giant, gaping yawn, giving the cavern another shake.

Sherry knew that when she had recently woken up, she'd rather not be bothered, but she also didn't want to miss her chance.

"Hey there!" she yelled as loud as her tiny voice could muster. The big lizard didn't notice. "Hey!" Sherry tried again. "Hey! Hey! Hey you!" Sherry was a little embarrassed, because yelling to get someone's attention seemed rather rude and she didn't want to be impolite, but it was the only thing she could think to do except perhaps throwing rocks, which was considerably more rude than yelling.

The lizard turned toward Sherry's small voice. He didn't spot her at first, but Sherry kept yelling and the lizard finally saw her. He climbed out of the lava and brought his head down near her.

"Oh, hello," he said. "You are very small. My name is Brim."

Sherry was relieved she wouldn't have to yell so much anymore. "Hello! My name is Sherry. You are very large. That's, um, kind of why I'm here, I suppose. I know you don't mean to cause a problem, but you are. My house is up there, and I'm worried you're going to knock it down."

"Your house is on the ceiling?" Brim asked. "Why on Earth would you build a house on the ceiling? That seems terribly unstable."

"No," Sherry said and shook her head. "My house is up on the surface, and when you roll around down here, it makes everything shake."

"But the surface is down here," Brim said, giving the ground a thump with his long, thick, tail. "See?"

"Oh," Sherry said. She thought for a moment, trying to figure out how to explain it. "I live, um, above the ceiling. The surface on the other side of it."

Brim's giant eyes grew even wider. "Above the ceiling? That's a place? You poor thing. It must be freezing up there so far away from this nice, soothing lava."

"It's, um, actually quite nice," Sherry said. "There's a sun and seasons and it's warm this time of year." She could see Brim was both curious and confused by this information, and she decided to stay focused on the matter at hand. "Anyway, when you roll around down here, it shakes everything up there, and I am very small. A small shake to you is a big shake to me. Probably to most everyone who lives where I do, honestly."

Brim let out a deep, concerned rumble. "I live here. I understand that you live there and I don't want to disturb anyone, but I can't just go away, either. The lava is right here. Could you go away?"

Sherry thought about it and then gave an honest answer. "I don't think so," she said. "When I was coming down here to meet you, there were cracks everywhere and a lot of smoke. I think I'd have to go *very* far away, and even if I could, there's all sorts of other creatures and people up there too. I don't think they could all move."

"Well, I don't know what to do," Brim rumbled.

The two of them thought about it for a long time. Sherry couldn't move everyone on the surface away, and Brim needed to stay near the lava. They thought for so long, Brim had another long nap and woke up again, and Sherry ate the rest of the food she had brought with her and started to get hungry. She wasn't sure what giant lava lizards liked to eat, but whatever it was, Sherry was fairly sure it wouldn't be good food for a mouse.

They both wanted to compromise, but no matter what they thought of, they couldn't solve the problem. They needed help.

"I'm very glad we met, but I need to return to the surface," Sherry finally said. "I even marked my way so I wouldn't get lost. And I'm not giving up, okay? I'm going to search far and wide until I find someone who can think of an answer. Then, I'll be back."

Brim nodded his enormous head in agreement. "And I'll try not to shake too much, although I'll still need to sometimes. I hope we can find something that works for us both."

"We will," Sherry promised. She was a determined and thoughtful mouse who was used to working on her own. In her heart, she knew she could solve any problem that came her way. No matter what happened, she wouldn't give up until she had exhausted every last possible option and given it her all. Sure, sometimes it could get frustrating, but that never seemed to help her succeed. Even if staying calm was sometimes difficult, it was always the best thing to do.

This time, though, she had a problem bigger than one mouse could handle. She knew that compromising was a good thing, and that it was okay to ask for help when you needed it. After all, no one could do everything alone! And even though Sherry didn't know it yet, help was on the way.

The Castle and the Cockatrice

Curio the cockatrice was not a beautiful animal. Everyone said so, and she agreed with them. She had a long, serpent body with hairy bat wings and big, bulky legs with even bigger feet. And on top of that, quite literally, she had a rooster's head that didn't match the rest of her *at all.*

To make matters worse, whenever she was sad or angry or scared, everyone around her turned to stone. And even though Curio was happy most of the time and tried her best to stay calm and be brave, everyone feels sad, angry, or scared sometimes. When that happened to Curio, *poof!* New friends would turn into solid statues, which was definitely a problem.

Curio played alone a lot of the time. It wasn't a great solution, because so many fun things to do were even more fun when you had a friend. Sometimes she would see other creatures playing tag or having a race, and Curio couldn't do that alone. Even things she could do alone, like eating lunch, going for walks, or digging for worms, would be more fun if someone else came along at least sometimes.

But Curio made the best of it. She found things she liked doing on her own, like reading or drawing. She liked using her imagination when things around her got boring.

From time to time, people came to visit Curio, and it was almost never good news. Sometimes, people would ask her to turn things to stone so they could build a house or a bridge and she was happy to help, but it was tiring. Sometimes, something would go missing and someone would accuse Curio of turning it to stone. She never did anything like that, at least not on purpose.

Sometimes, people would tell her to leave, and that was the worst. She didn't want to leave her home and she didn't have anywhere else to go, anyway. Curio ignored those people the best she could—especially because if she didn't, they usually got turned to stone, and she didn't want that either.

One day, however, was different. Curio was alone in her yard practicing some dance moves (she wasn't a very good dancer, but it was fun anyway) when someone she had never seen approached. He was tall, with pink skin and very fancy clothes. They were bright red and purple and Curio didn't see dirt on them *anywhere*. It was hard to imagine someone being that careful all the time.

"Hello, cockatrice," the man said when he saw her. "I come with an urgent request from the king."

The king? Curio had heard of him, but the way people spoke about him living far away in a grand palace, Curio was never quite sure if he was actually real or just a tall tale. Apparently there was, in fact, a real king.

"I'm happy to help," Curio told the messenger. "Although I'm not really sure how I could."

"I'm told you're the perfect person for the job. Please come with me," he said.

That surprised Curio. She had never been the perfect person for anything before. She felt like there must be some mistake, but she didn't want to miss an opportunity either, so they began their journey.

It was much more pleasant than Curio expected. She had imagined a long and tiring walk, but instead she was led to a large, beautiful brown carriage pulled by two even more beautiful white horses. Curio said hello to them, but they took their job very seriously and didn't respond.

"I suppose when you work for the king, you travel in style," Curio remarked.

"Of course," the messenger replied, helping her into the carriage. The inside of the carriage was just as wonderful as the outside, with red velvet seats and pillows. Curio had never felt something so soft and comfortable.

"Will I get to meet the king?" she asked.

The messenger shifted in his seat, suddenly nervous. "I should think not," he said. "I mean, no offense. But accidentally turning a king to stone simply wouldn't do."

No, of course not, Curio thought. She felt foolish, and although she remained calm, she was quiet for the rest of the ride.

When they finally arrived at the castle, Curio was surprised. She had always heard that kings lived in mighty and majestic castles, but this castle was nothing like she'd imagined. It wasn't *horrible,* but it was rather small. Curio could see that it had once been larger, but some of the walls had crumbled and other parts were abandoned, with moss and vines growing over them. It would take more than a good cleaning to restore this castle to its former glory.

I get it, Curio thought. *I'm here to restore the castle. That's all I'm good for, turning things to stone.* It was a saddening thought. She didn't mind helping, but she wished she had the opportunity to be something more. She was a whole person who liked a lot of different things, not just a rock-making factory. She was good at that, but didn't the world already have enough rocks? Curio liked to be around people, but after this, maybe she would go live alone in the forest so she wouldn't be bothered.

Curio could feel the sadness inside her rising up and she knew that any moment, it would burst out of her and turn the messenger and the horses to stone. She didn't want that. She *really* didn't want that. It was hard to control, but she took some deep breaths and imagined floating away somewhere peaceful until she started to feel better. Slowly, Curio became more calm. She would talk about how she felt with someone when she had the chance.

"Right this way, please," the messenger said, interrupting her thoughts. He opened the door of the carriage for Curio. She thought he looked rather out of place, clean and polished among the run-down castle. He must work very hard to keep his spirits up. Maybe controlling his emotions was hard for him sometimes, too.

The inside of the castle was odd. Sometimes they would pass a vase of bright and beautiful flowers, while other times, they would pass one that was wilted. Sometimes they would pass a beautiful tapestry with an ornate design, and other times they would pass one that was old and dusty and dirty. The same was true for everything else—it looked like people were trying very hard to keep things bright and beautiful, but had too much work to do and couldn't keep up.

The messenger led Curio through the halls and up a long, spiral staircase. There were candleholders on the walls, but most of them were empty. The few candles that remained were unlit, so they walked in darkness except for an occasional window slit. When a ray of sunlight shot through into the castle, Curio could see the many dust particles floating in the air.

They reached the top of the stairs and a heavy wooden door. The messenger gave it the gentlest of knocks. There was no answer.

"Princess Persephone, it is your humble servant," the messenger said. "May I enter?"

"No, you may not," a voice said from behind the door. The words came out slowly, one at a time, with a long pause between each. It wasn't mean or angry or forceful, but it carried an air of authority.

The messenger paused for a moment, considering. Then he said, "I have a visitor for you who's come quite a long way."

"Fine," the princess allowed. "Enter if you must." The words came out one at a time again, with a moment of silence between each. Curio even thought they should go in after the princess said "enter," but the messenger was patient and let the princess finish her thought.

Curio wondered why the messenger would be so protective of the king, but not protective of the princess. Curio resolved, then and there, that no matter what happened she would not turn the princess into stone.

She didn't need to worry for long. The messenger opened the door, and the princess was waiting for them in the center of the room.

She was stunning, with a caring smile and a long, intricate dress. She was also made of solid stone.

Her hair was delicate: very fine and more beautiful and detailed than any mason could create, but it did not move, because it was stone. Her skin, her clothes, her slippers, everything… all of it smooth, gray stone. She even had delicate stone eyelashes atop her stone gray eyes.

"How may I help you, visitor?" Princess Persephone asked. Curio was shocked to see that the princess could indeed move, although very slowly and with great effort. Now she understood why the words were coming out so differently. It must be difficult to speak when you were made of stone. Curio resolved to be extra patient.

"I'm not really sure," Curio admitted. "The messenger asked me to come, so I did."

The messenger responded quickly. "Princess Persephone, this is a cockatrice, and I searched far and wide to find her. I thought you might enjoy her presence."

"I see," said Persephone. "I will meet with our visitor. You, however, may go."

The messenger bowed and left the room, shutting the door and leaving Curio alone with the princess.

"I'm terribly sorry," Curio said. "But I'm rather confused. The messenger said he would like me to come here at the request of the king, but he was otherwise quite unclear."

"I apologize on his behalf," the princess said. "He means well, but when he gets an idea in his head, he gets so focused that he forgets to explain himself. Make yourself comfortable and I'll do it for him."

Curio obeyed, finding a soft pillow and settling in to hear the story.

"Where to begin?" the princess wondered out loud. It was clear it was a labor to speak, and Curio did not rush her. "My father's messenger is in the habit of bringing me all manner of things in an attempt to cheer me up."

Curio looked around. She had been so enchanted by the stone princess that she hadn't noticed the oddities littering the room. There were jewels and coins and games with ornate pieces. There were paintings and seashells and sparkling crowns—everything Curio could imagine and several things she couldn't. By the look of it, it was all untouched.

"A fairy put a curse on my mother, Queen Ana, and said her daughter would turn to stone. That was me. Later she went to bargain with the fairy to fix things, but she never returned. My father has been sad ever since, and things have fallen into disrepair."

"That's awful," Curio said.

"Sometimes bad things happen, and this time, they happened to us." Persephone shrugged her shoulders sadly.

"I don't have any friends," Curio said. "I turn people to stone sometimes, by accident, so people avoid me." Then she realized what the messenger had in mind. "Could I stay a while, and play with you? I don't think I could turn you to stone, because, well…"

Princess Persephone laughed. It was sweet and musical and reminded Curio of wind chimes. Curio wondered if her laugh had always been like that, or if it was part of the fairy curse. Either way, Curio liked it a lot.

At first they talked a lot, sharing the stories of their lives. Sometimes, Princess Persephone didn't feel like talking, so they read books together or played games quietly. They explored Persephone's room of curiosities and had all manner of fun.

Curio enjoyed being with Persephone so much, she asked the messenger to return to her home and gather her things so she could live in the castle. Some days they played together all day, and sometimes only a little.

Persephone and Curio practiced together, with Persephone encouraging Curio to control her stone-freezing powers and Curio encouraging Persephone to move around as much as she could. It wasn't easy and they weren't perfect, but they were better together than they were alone.

The princess's laughter filled the castle more days than not, and the king's spirits lifted as well. He even hired more workers to fix up the castle and help with the work he couldn't do himself. Slowly, with much effort, the castle transformed from a dusty wreck into a bright and welcoming place people came from all around to visit.

Curio was glad she had been patient and didn't rush to conclusions. She had almost declined to come with the messenger and then almost abandoned her trip when she thought she was being used for her stone-making powers. If she hadn't been generous in assuming the best about the messenger, she never would have met a lifelong friend. Curio knew she had to be cautious, but that wouldn't stop her from being kind.

The pair of them stayed together for a long time after that. Sometimes Curio and Persephone were happy, and sometimes they were sad. But they were together, and that made them both feel better. Because sometimes it can be really difficult to find friends who truly understand you, and it can be really hard to wait until you do. But when you find the people who match you just right, well—that's something really special.

The Sky Queen and Her Many Subjects

Being the queen of Artasia was a very important job, and Queen Kiria took it very seriously. It was her responsibility to manage everyone and everything in Artasia, from shaping the buildings to preparing the festivals to making sure everyone got to bed on time but still had enough fun to be happy. On top of that, it was her job to make sure the weather was just right for all the people in the world below, because Artasia was a kingdom in the sky.

Rain, snow, fog, and sunshine were all up to Queen Kiria. Would it be warm or cold? A cloudy day or a sunny one? Would the people in the world below see the moon and the stars that night, or would they have to wait? Whether it was a tiny spring breeze, a mighty hurricane, or anything else in between, every tiny detail was up to her.

At first, when the world was new, Queen Kiria liked her job. But as more and more people spread out all over the world, her job got more and more difficult. Elves liked warm weather and dwarves liked cold weather. The frogs and bugs liked things nice and wet, and the giants and sandworms liked things very dry. Goblins and fairies never wanted the same weather twice, yet never seemed to agree with each other either. Honestly, it was a mess.

However, all of them relied on Queen Kiria, even if most of them didn't even realize that the kingdom of Artasia existed. So she worked hard, day after day and night after night. She was satisfied with her efforts, inventing the seasons and all their wonders along with all the different kinds of weather. But she was never finished. She was sure she had rested sometime in the past, but she couldn't remember when.

She sat in her palace made of clouds. Someone in the world down below might say, "Hey, that cloud looks like a castle!" But it was a cloud too, and they would never guess she lived inside it. Some creatures liked looking at the clouds a lot. Queen Kiria would shape the clouds like a bird or a puppy or a smile on purpose just to make those creatures happy.

Today, she had more important tasks at hand. A tiny tornado of clouds whipped into the throne room and one of her cloud servants appeared. Sometimes, she would send a gust of wind to make them disappear, and they would re-form from the clouds with a laugh. But today, she was in no mood to play around.

"My queen." The servant bowed. "There was too much rain near the eastern forest, and I'm afraid it caused a flood. The mermaids are happy, but the dryads are *quite* distressed."

Well, that certainly wasn't ideal. It would take a lot of careful changes to clear things up, which meant it would take a lot of her attention. It was frustrating. There was always something or another.

"If I may, Your Majesty?" the servant asked.

"You may not," Queen Kiria said. "I'll handle it."

Kiria was sure that the servant would remark that she looked tired. It was true. But then he would ask her if he should take care of it himself, and she didn't want that. She suspected some of her servants might be taking care of things themselves already. But if she didn't do it herself, how could she be sure it would get done correctly?

Kiria waved a hand and a cloud rushed around her. When it blew away, she was gone. Her magic swept her away so she could take a closer look at the flooding. She was still high in the clouds, but now she was close enough to see the damage for herself.

"Oh no," she said. The damage was even worse than the messenger had explained. The river had swollen well past its banks, and the rushing water had destroyed many trees. Some of them were partially ripped out by the roots. Others were fully toppled on their sides. And by the look of things, some of them had been swept away altogether.

"Well, I can understand why the dryads are so upset," Queen Kiria muttered to herself. "And I have no one to blame but myself."

Kiria got started immediately, pushing the clouds out of the sky and calling the sun to beam down hotly. She slowed the winds to a gentle breeze, then changed her mind and let the wind blow a bit harder. The sun would make the water evaporate, and then the wind could carry it away. The mermaids would be a bit less happy. The dryads would still need to replant their trees. It was exhausting, but it was the best she could do. She resolved to check on things again in a day or two.

Kiria waved a hand again, and her magic carried her back to her palace. She was far too busy to sleep, but maybe she could at least sit down for a moment.

To her surprise, several of her servants had assembled in the throne room. Her daughters, the princesses Nadia, Cora, Ravea, and Shine, waited with them. Queen Kiria had had a very long, very tiring day, and she was absolutely, positively, not in the mood for nonsense.

"Oh, come now," Queen Kiria said dismissively. "There cannot *possibly* be this many problems all at once. Unless you have a problem right at this very moment, please leave."

No one moved. The queen's four daughters stepped forward, their faces showing concern. They each looked like their mother in their own way, with sky blue eyes, rainbows in their hair, and gowns made of trailing clouds. Only Shine was a little different. Her name was no accident, as she glowed with a yellow light of her own that got more intense when she had strong feelings. This evening, she lit the entire palace so brightly that the creatures on the ground might begin to wonder what was happening.

"Mother, we love you and we are glad to see you," Shine began. "But we are worried. Your work has become very challenging, and it is clearly too much."

Shine was always the daughter who spoke most directly. Queen Kiria's eyes narrowed.

"Are you saying I am not up to the task of ruling my kingdom?" she asked.

Princess Cora stepped forward. "Not at all, mother. But it is okay to rest, and you have earned it. We would like to give you that rest, so you can be refreshed." She could see she was not getting through to the queen. "As a gift?" she added hopefully.

Princess Nadia could see her sisters' pleas were not working. "Mother," she begged. "You have so many servants, and all of them are happy to be of service. Why not let them? What good is it to surround yourself with so many helpful people, if you won't let them be of any help?"

The truth was, even though she was a queen, Kiria was ashamed to ask for help. She was powerful and mighty, and asking for others' help made her worry she would seem weak. She didn't want to be weak, especially not around people she cared about. And she loved them, every last one. She didn't want to burden them.

Queen Kiria let out a long sigh and sank onto her throne. "You are my subjects. You are my family. I don't want to make things harder for you."

Ravea, the gentlest of the princesses, spoke for them all. "We *are* family, mother. We want to help you when we can. If it becomes too difficult, we will be honest and get the help we need. Everyone can be happier if we all work together. You don't have to work alone."

Queen Kiria knew they were right. "I will agree to ask for help, only if you do the same. It is not a daughter's responsibility to care for her mother. It is a mother's responsibility to care for her daughters. I will let you help tend to my kingdom, but you must agree to ask for assistance if you ever need it."

"Yes, mother," they all agreed.

Queen Kiria divided up the kingdom, and each daughter was left in charge of something different. Clever Cora was tasked with watching the rain and snow. Steadfast Nadia moved the seasons, one to the next. Gentle Ravea would guide the clouds. And radiant Shine would call the sun and moon and stars.

None of them was as mighty or capable as their mother. But they worked together, they asked for help, and a great many cloud people helped them as well. Keeping everyone together was still challenging in its own way, but Queen Kiria gave her best effort and asked for help as well when she needed it. And since they were all working together, she was finally able to get some rest.

A Goblin Unlike Any Other

Goblins, by nature, are loud and easily excited little creatures. They love to dance and sing and crash things together. They play, eat, work, and sleep in noisy, chaotic groups. Goblins mean well, but often can't help themselves and end up causing trouble, which leads to them laughing and jumping around and generally being even louder and more chaotic. Pinn was not like other goblins, and she liked it that way.

Pinn didn't dislike the other goblins, and she thought it was okay that they were themselves and did what made them happy. She liked to watch them and their antics, but it was rare that she joined in. She liked to read and study and think about interesting plants and animals, math formulas she found in old books, or fanciful adventures. But she liked things most when there was peace and quiet. Her parents and friends often remarked, not unkindly, that she was the quietest goblin that there ever was—and they were right.

Today, Pinn was organizing her leaf collection, which she had dried between the pages of a book she didn't need anymore. Then she was going to practice her handwriting, which was an unusual skill for a goblin, but she enjoyed it. Finally, if she had time, she would look for an ant hill to study—being very careful not to disturb the ants. Just because Pinn was quiet didn't mean she wasn't busy.

The problem was, the other goblins had other ideas. Not all the same idea, mind you, but each had their own ideas, just like Pinn. There were all manner of acrobatics, wrestling, kite flying, soup making, digging, jumping, building... anything you could imagine, a goblin was busy doing. The one thing they all seemed to have in common was that they were very, very, loud. On top of it all, the ground rumbled occasionally. Pinn was pretty sure that wasn't the goblins' fault, but it was still annoying.

Pinn did her best to stay calm. Sometimes she was successful, and sometimes she wasn't. She wanted every goblin to be happy and do the things they liked, but it was all so... overwhelming. Some days she was able to find a quiet place to be alone. Today, though, she was not so lucky.

A group of goblins played a game in a nearby field, kicking a ball around. Sometimes they would kick the ball so hard and so far it would bounce over to her. Since there were no boundaries to the game, the goblins would gleefully crash over to her, chasing the ball and filling her space with dust and noise. Sometimes, they even did it on purpose. It wasn't because they were mean, Pinn knew, but because they thought she would want to play and be noisy with them. Goblins are a lot of wonderful things, but they are not very observant.

The ball flew toward Pinn, landing on one of her very favorite leaves and crushing it. She had had enough. "Stop, stop, stop!" she cried, scooping up the rest of her leaves just before the other goblins crashed over to her.

"Stop it, you loud little meanies!" Pinn yelled at them, kicking clouds of dirt at them. "Can't you be quiet for even one minute? Do you have to be loud every second of every day?"

This made the other goblins pause. They looked at each other, confused by the question.

"Yes?" one offered.

"Why not?" said another.

"I think so," said a third.

The other goblins nodded and chattered in agreement, and in a moment, they were all as loud as ever.

Pinn threw her hands up in frustration. She didn't know what else to say, and the other goblins weren't listening, anyway. She stomped away from them as far as her legs could carry her. This concerned the rest of the goblins, but they let her go.

She walked and walked until everyone else was out of sight. She felt relieved. The wind was blowing and the birds were singing. Pinn didn't mind these sounds, because they were quiet and soothing. Expected. Predictable. Peaceful. Pinn felt herself becoming calmer.

Pinn was lucky enough to find a large anthill bustling with many workers. They marched in and out, each on their own but also together. She even spotted one carrying a leaf she liked.

"Why can't goblins be like that?" Pinn wondered. "You don't have to be noisy to find lots of things to do."

The day stretched onward as the sun soared high in the sky. Pinn had enough of watching the ants and moved on to picking flowers, then climbing trees. She did find that it was less interesting without the other goblins around, even if it was more peaceful.

Before too long, though, the other goblins came looking for Pinn. Lost in her thoughts, she heard them before she saw them. They tried to be quiet as they approached, but they weren't very good at it.

The group stopped well short of Pinn, giving her space. There was a bit of a commotion, and then one of the smaller goblins was pushed toward.

"Hi, Pinn," the little goblin stammered. "I'm sorry to bother you, but we'd really like it if you came back. I know it might not feel like it sometimes, but we really like having you around. Um, really!"

It was clear the little goblin was very nervous, and Pinn thought he was very brave for speaking up. But even though he was being brave and didn't mean any harm, Pinn wasn't sure she was ready to return.

"I like watching you," Pinn said. "And sometimes I even like playing with you. But everything is so noisy, and it really bothers me. It makes me feel strange inside and I need to run away. I like you all but I can't be around you when you act like that." Pinn thought she was perhaps being unkind, so she added, "I understand that you want to play and that's okay, but I still just… can't."

The little goblin wasn't sure how to respond, so he ran back to the rest of the group. They put their heads together and spoke rapidly, talking over each other in typical goblin fashion. After a few minutes, the talking slowly stopped, and the little goblin emerged from the group a second time.

"We can't really be quiet," the little goblin admitted. "We tried really hard but I just don't think we can. At least not very much. Sometimes. Maybe. A little." He looked embarrassed by this admission. "But we have an idea. You wait here, and we'll come back later, okay?"

"Okay," Pinn agreed. She was curious about what the other goblins had planned, but she suspected that if she asked, it would cause another chaotic huddle. She decided it was best for all involved if she just waited.

The goblins left, and Pinn amused herself by reading a storybook about a magical sky queen. She wondered what it would be like to live in the sky and if it was peaceful up there, or if it was very busy. She decided she might like to try and live in the sky, as long as she could come back down if she didn't like it.

Pinn read until the sun was about to set. She wanted to wait for her goblin friends, but she needed to get home before dark. Had they forgotten about her? Goblins were easily distracted—there was no denying that—but they always got back around to things when they remembered.

It turned out that Pinn didn't need to worry, after all. The others returned right as she was about ready to give up, and this time, they were even worse at containing their excitement. Now they all wanted to talk to her.

"Come with us!" one yelled.

"Hurry, so we can show you right away!" called another.

"You're going to love it!" shouted a third. After that, so many goblins were talking at once it was impossible to make out what they were saying. After a long day of peace and quiet, Pinn felt ready to go with them and wasn't bothered too much.

They led Pinn past the field where they usually played to a large tree that was a good distance away, but still visible from the field. When Pinn got closer, she saw that the other goblins had built something. Planks of wood were nailed to the tree to make a ladder up into the branches. At the end of the ladder was a tree house. It had windows on every side and even a bright pink flag. The most special thing, however, was the sign nailed next to the doorway, which read "Pin's Quiet Place." (Pinn would add the extra "n" later when she had a chance. Most goblins aren't very good at spelling, but that's okay.)

"Thank you?" Pinn said quizzically.

"Now you can go up in your treehouse when you want things to be quieter," one of the goblins explained. "We even tried it ourselves, and it's pretty quiet up there. Not perfectly quiet, but it was a good try. And you said you still liked to watch us play, so there's a lot of windows, and you can see the whole field from up there."

"That's amazing," Pinn said, happy that her friends had been so thoughtful. "Thank you," she said again.

One of the other goblins spoke up. "Plus, we all decided that when we did come over to see you, we would do our best to be quiet. The sign reminds us! Then, when we can't be quiet any longer, we can always run off somewhere else."

And so it was that Pinn was able to live happily with the other goblins. At first, she mostly sat in her treehouse. But because she had a quiet place of her own to retreat to, she was able to relax. She started coming down to play more often, and the other goblins tried very hard to be quiet when they visited her.

Sometimes, no one is right or wrong. But if you talk about what you need and everyone listens, you can show you care by finding something that works for everyone. It's always okay to ask for what you need, whether you're a goblin or any other kind of creature.

The Flower Maze

Ask anyone, and they'll tell you that Minotaurs are scary monsters. It's not hard to see why. They have hairy legs and torsos, plus hooves and long, swishing tails. Their upper body looks like a human, but with more muscles than a human could ever have, and it's topped by a bull's head with giant, sharp horns.

Minotaurs need a lot of space to themselves, so they live alone, or rarely in pairs. They visit each other from time to time, but not very often.

Visiting a Minotaur is a real challenge. One thing every Minotaur has in common is living in confusing mazes. Most Minotaurs live in mazes made of stone, or in a network of underground caves. Sometimes they even live in castle dungeons, if the builders made them big and confusing enough. (The more confusing, the better.)

Molly the Minotaur was no exception. She loved to get lost in a maze and admire the walls. Sometimes they were made of brick, sometimes of stone. She had even heard of mazes made of corn, although she had never visited one. There were only two things Molly liked more than visiting mazes: building mazes and flowers.

Now, building mazes, Molly's family understood. That was a very Minotaur sort of thing to do. A tradition as far back as any Minotaur could remember. The flowers, though... those were a problem.

Molly's brother Garonar was over for a visit, and he was talking about the flowers again, like he did every time he visited. "Minotaurs are strong," he said. "And our mazes are supposed to be strong, too. Stone. Steel. Bone. *Anything* would be stronger than flowers. I could have walked right through them if I wanted to. I only followed the maze paths because I am so polite."

Molly did not think criticizing something she loved was very polite, and it frustrated her to have the same conversation again and again. "For the record," she pointed out, "I am stronger than you are. And my maze doesn't need to be strong. I want my maze to be beautiful, and it is. It's the way I like it."

Garonar huffed. He stomped around the living room while he talked, a habit he'd had as a child. He was always moving. "What about protection? Anyone could come in here if they wanted to. You never know who might come along."

Molly waved a hand at him dismissively. "Oh, hush. People used to bother Minotaurs, sure. But that almost never happens anymore, and not here. I'm in no danger. And if someone tried to bother me, *they* would be in danger." She flexed her powerful muscles in demonstration. "If it's so dangerous over by your maze, why not come live with me? I can show you how to tend the gardens."

Garonar laughed. It was a big, thundering laugh that scattered the birds outside. Molly laughed too. They were very different from each other, but they were still siblings and friends. They knew neither would change all that much.

"Let's go outside," Garonar offered. "I don't want any flowers of my own, but I'll enjoy yours while I'm here."

They went outside and sat on the ground among the flowers. Garonar sneezed. It was a great, booming sneeze that made the flowers bend away from him and scared off the squirrels who played in the yard. The flowers always made him sneeze. He had to admit, however, that they were very beautiful.

Molly and Garonar talked about their lives, because as solitary creatures they didn't visit each other very often. Garonar talked about lining his cave with torches to give it a spooky, shadowy glow. Molly talked about building a birdhouse and a feeder to attract more animals. She had recently enticed some rabbits to visit her, and she liked that.

Garonar always felt uneasy when he wasn't tucked away in the safety of his own maze. He was just starting to relax and enjoy the day when he stopped talking and sniffed the air.

"Knight," he whispered. "I know it."

"Oh, hogwash," Molly said in a normal voice. She stopped and sniffed the air. There was definitely something strange. She really hoped it wasn't a knight. She would never hear the end of it.

Garonar paced around the garden, tilting his head this way and that, trying to hear the intruder. He flared his nostrils. He swished his tail. He stomped his feet. Molly hoped again that it wasn't a knight looking for trouble. If it was, Molly had a feeling it wouldn't end well for them.

After waiting for what seemed like forever, a very small figure in a very tall hat appeared from the maze. "That really was an adventure and a half, wasn't it? You've been working really hard on all those flowers. I'll admit it, for a minute— floating boats and buttered toast, there's two of you now!"

Garonar roared. It was the fiercest, mightiest roar the gnome had ever heard, and she ran for her life. There was a large clatter as she dropped all manner of pots and pans as she ran. Her tall, pointed hat flew off immediately.

"Wait, wait, wait!" Molly called, more to Garonar than the gnome.

Garonar didn't listen. Couldn't listen, really. He saw a threat and all he could think about was protecting his sister. Molly grabbed him and wrestled him down. It wasn't easy, and they crushed several perfectly good flowers as they wrestled. But it was true that Molly was stronger than her brother, and eventually he gave up.

"That's not a knight," Molly said, panting for breath. She still held on to Garonar with all her strength. "That's my friend Terrin the gnome. It smelled like metal because she was coming over to cook and brought all her cookware. That's my guess, anyway. I think you scared her so much we may never find her."

Garonar struggled against his sister, although at this point it was more for his pride than anything else. "You have friends who aren't Minotaurs?" he asked. "Mom and Dad are going to have a fit."

"Well, then, Mom and Dad need to get over it," Molly said. She gave Garonar one more hard squeeze and let him up. "She's nice and I like her. And she's harmless. Except for her apple cobbler, which is positively dangerous. You could eat six of them."

"You can come back, Terrin!" Molly called out, her voice carrying over the entire garden. "It's safe, I promise!"

Molly busied herself inspecting the poor flowers that had been damaged during the fight. She selected some that had broken from their stems to make a bouquet. Garonar apologized and looked rather embarrassed, so Molly didn't complain or tease him about it.

Terrin made an appearance once she had regathered all the things she'd thrown aside, and she was indeed there to make apple cobbler. Garonar was doubtful at first, but the delicious dessert won him over. They talked long into the night, and Garonar was enchanted by the little gnome. Terrin had stories he had never heard and jokes that surprised him. Along with more and more apple cobbler, of course. There was just so much joy to be had in meeting new and different people, even for someone as particular and set in their ways as a Minotaur.

There were times when Molly still got questioned by other well-meaning Minotaurs. They didn't get it when she told them about things she loved. But to Molly, those other Minotaurs didn't need to understand. Not really. She loved the things she loved, and she was confident in that. She was much happier being herself than trying to be someone else.

The Obsidian Castle

The rumbling throughout the land had become completely unmanageable. The mice's homes were in shambles. The king and his workers struggled to keep the castle walls standing. The goblins shrieked and ran around with every rumble, making things worse. Even the trees in the great forest were concerned for their roots.

Wist had never seen anything like it—so many different creatures all in the same place. An elf and a dwarf sat together discussing the problem. The king's messenger was in a heated argument with a giant Minotaur. Farmers scolded a pair of dryads for not helping things grow. The goblins ran from group to group making themselves everybody's problem. And no one would listen to the mice, no matter how hard they tried to attract attention.

Wist sympathized with the mice, as she too couldn't get anyone to listen. The elf dismissed her because she was so young. The Minotaur said she was too small, and the king's messenger called her naive, which is what adults called her when they didn't want to take her seriously. The farmers told her to run along, and the dryads were so upset they didn't respond to her at all.

A mouse pulled on the leg of Wist's pants. It was hard to hear her over the commotion, so Wist bent down close to her.

"I know what the problem is, but no one will listen!" said the mouse. Wist understood. She felt like that sometimes, too.

"I'm listening!" Wist replied. "It's nice to meet you."

The mouse tipped her tiny hat in greeting. "There's a big lava lizard under the ground," she said. "He's not dangerous or anything, but when he splashes around in his lava, everything shakes."

Wist was concerned. "How big are we talking here?"

The mouse looked around for something to compare it to. "I'd say ten Minotaurs, maybe? At least."

Wist's eyes went wide. "That sounds pretty dangerous to me," she said.

A goblin ran past, interrupting them. The mouse tried to speak again, but two more goblins ran after the first, stopping her again. Checking to make sure there weren't any more of them giving chase, she continued. "I'm sure. I talked to him for a long time, and he really doesn't want to cause trouble. I would have been in big trouble, if he decided to be mean."

"Can we ask him to stop?" Wist asked.

The mouse shook her head. "He tried, but he can't stay still all the time. Imagine how impossible that would be." The ground let out a great rumble as if to confirm the mouse's tale.

"Can we talk to him now?" Wist asked.

"I don't think so," the mouse said. "The tunnel that took me to him was very small, and I had to walk a long time. And with all the shaking, I don't even know if the tunnels would still be open."

Wist nodded. She looked around; they were getting nowhere. The rumble had made everyone pause for a moment, but then they went back to arguing.

"Hey, everybody!" Wist yelled as loud as she could. No one listened.

"Everybody, I'm going to try something!" she yelled again. Still nothing.

"Okay, it's going to happen, so everyone look out!" It was like she wasn't even there. "Well, fine," she said.

Wist scooped the mouse up onto her shoulder. "Come with me. My name is Wist, by the way."

The mouse replied, "My name is Sherry. Thanks for the ride."

Wist jogged a fair distance away from the group, then took her walking stick and pushed it into the dirt. Sherry looked on curiously, but she didn't interrupt.

"Beauty, I don't know if you can hear me, but I know your voice carried very far, so I hope you can. I need your help, and no one else is mighty enough. A lizard is trapped in the earth far below us, and I'd like to let him out."

Sherry squeaked in surprise. Nothing happened at first, and then the wind started to blow. Ever so faintly, both of them heard, "You are loved. All of you."

The ground began to shake.

The earth around Wist and Sherry began to crumble away until they were standing on a tiny island in the middle of the field. Wist grabbed the walking stick, jumped across to the solid ground, and ran.

The hole got bigger, and bigger, and bigger. The others watched in confusion for a moment, and then they ran, too. Luckily, everyone was too busy running to see that Wist was the one who had made the hole, or she would be in some serious trouble. She might be in trouble later anyway if this didn't work out.

The hole finally stopped growing, and there was silence as everyone tried to figure out what had happened. Even the goblins were stunned. No one was hurt, though. Wist suspected that Beauty had been careful in that regard. Dust hung in the air. Otherwise, it was quite peaceful—calm, even. Then, the lava lizard popped out.

Wist wasn't sure who screamed first, but once someone did, everyone started screaming. Some of them ran in terror, others hid, and a few of them looked ready to fight. When the beast lumbered out of the hole, Wist could see he was *definitely* bigger than ten Minotaurs. Wist didn't say anything to her new friend Sherry about it. Sherry could see it too.

"Well, what do you know?" the lizard said. "It really *is* nice up here. Hi, everyone. My name's Brim."

No one was sure what to say in response, so Wist took charge. She trusted Sherry and got as close as she could, waving for Brim's attention. "Hi up there!" she yelled. "My name is Wist Willowflower. Sorry about the big hole."

Brim brought his head down close to Wist. "Hello, Wist Willowflower. I don't mind the hole at all, because now I can get a good stretch." He noticed the mouse on Wist's shoulder. "Oh, hi again, Sherry. Did you find the help we needed?"

"I think so," Sherry said. "At least I hope so, or we're going to have a lot of explaining to do."

Smoke had begun billowing out of the hole. Wist could see some of the people using their shirt or a piece of cloth to cover their noses and mouths. It was a pretty powerful smell for someone who wasn't used to it.

"Sorry about that," Brim said."Not much I can do about that. There's a *lot* of lava down there. Great for a swim, actually."

Wist was having fun meeting a new friend, but she knew she had to think fast. "Is it okay if we build you a castle? Like, a big house. We could build it on top of the hole, and then you could stay there, nice and warm, with all the lava underneath. Then you wouldn't have to shake the ground as much when you moved around. You could even come out and lay in the grass on warm days."

"Positively wonderful," Brim said.

Wist left Sherry with Brim and went over to the king's messenger. He hadn't introduced himself to her, but she could guess who he was, because he looked very fancy. "Hey there, Mr. Messenger Fancy Pants," she said. The messenger looked quite pleased at having his wardrobe complimented. "You work for the king, right? Or a duke, or a lord, or someone in a castle anyway."

"Yes, I work for the king," the messenger replied stiffly. "It's a very important job."

Wist nodded. She wanted to point out that lots of jobs were important jobs, but this wasn't the time. "Well, kings live in castles, which means you know how to build a castle, or you know how to find someone who does. I need you to build a castle right there over that hole."

The messenger was shocked. "I… excuse me, you're a little girl, right? You can't just order a whole castle. Not only a castle, but the biggest castle I've ever seen."

"Yes, I am a little girl," Wist said proudly. "But just because I'm a little girl doesn't mean I don't have big ideas. And this is a good one. The lizard can live in the castle, the lava will keep it warm, and the walls and tall chimneys will keep the smoke from getting everywhere. No more earthquakes. Problem solved." She snapped a finger.

If only it were that simple.

The messenger finally agreed to take her idea back to the king, and the king admitted it was a good plan. (He also asked the messenger to offer Wist a job as his royal advisor, which she politely declined.) The messenger returned with all the workers he could find, as well as Curio the cockatrice. They would need a lot of stone for this job.

Curio could turn anything she wanted into stone. She'd gotten a lot better at controlling her powers, much to the relief of everyone involved. The workers started with the stone they could find, and then Curio turned more and more things into rock. Trees, bread, old clothes, stuffed animals, bales of hay, anything people could bring to her. The job was long and tiring.

And it still wasn't working. The heat from the lava below kept melting the rock. Not quickly, since rock is pretty durable stuff, but slowly and surely. They would build a wall, and it would melt together, and then start to droop, and finally fall into the hole. Wist wasn't ready to give up yet, but she was becoming very discouraged. Brim was more patient, but Wist could tell he was worried too.

Luckily, Wist had one more person looking after her—someone she had never even met. Kiria the sky queen had been watching as the many people below her tried their very best to work together, and she was impressed. She wanted to make sure everyone could keep getting along, so she decided to help.

Wist saw her coming, as the queen rode down on a white cloud trailing a beautiful sparkling rainbow. She lowered herself toward the ground slowly, although she didn't touch it. "Hello, young queen," she said. "I am Kiria, Queen of the Kingdom of Artasia, which you call the sky."

"Pleased to meet you," Wist said with a bow. "Although I must admit I am not a queen." Wist had met so many amazing people recently, and they all seemed to have an idea of which job she should be doing. She knew it was coming from a place of kindness, but it solidified her desire to find her own way.

"My apologies," Queen Kiria said. It was an easy mistake to make, since the many workers had gotten into the habit of asking Wist for instructions about what to do next. Kiria was not used to a land where everyone could work together without being commanded by a queen. "I am here to help."

"We could certainly use some," Wist said. "We've got a good idea and we're all working hard, but it's not coming together. That happens sometimes and my mother says that's okay, but this time it's *really* important."

"Build your castle, and I will do the rest," Kiria commanded. Then she added, "And tell your workers to bring their coats and hats and gloves."

It was a strange thing to ask, but it was far from the strangest thing Wist had experienced recently, so she passed the warning on to the workers. They too had grown used to many strange happenings, so they got ready.

They built the castle walls again, sweating in their coats and hats due to the summer weather and the lava below them heating up the rocks. They were so warm they wouldn't be able to keep this up for long. Maybe it was time to stop and have some ice cream, or a swim in a nice, cold lake. But as tempting as it was, they didn't give up.

And then it started to snow.

It fell slowly at first, a few light snowflakes that melted when they got close, so small and fleeting that the workers thought their minds were playing tricks on them. But before long, it was a mighty blizzard with icy rain mixed in for good measure.

The goblins ran around trying to catch the snow on their tongues, and before long a snowball fight broke out. After so much warmth, everyone was in high spirits. (Brim decided it was a good time to go back underground for a bit, but he had plenty of lava to keep him warm.)

Most importantly, the walls of the castle sizzled and steamed as they cooled rapidly. Before long, Brim could splash lava up on the interior of the walls, where the snow and rain quickly turned it into smooth, hard obsidian. The steam and smoke rose into the air, but Kiria used strong winds to carry it away. Soon, the walls hardened into a beautiful, black fortress where Brim would be able to relax without fear that the walls would melt.

Everyone looked happy except for the Minotaur, who Wist had learned was named Molly. Molly had been so helpful for the entire project. She tirelessly carried material with her giant muscles, doing the work of thirty men.

"What's the matter, Molly?" Wist asked. "Aren't you happy the castle is almost finished? You worked so hard on it, after all."

"I'm happy for Brim," Molly said. "But what I really love is flowers and gardens and giant mazes. I was hoping that when the castle was finished I could make a huge flower garden here to surround it, but I don't think it's going to work. There's still a lot of smoke coming out of the castle's chimneys, and we can't ask Queen Kiria to stay here all the time. Plus, if I'm being honest, there are an awful lot of people around. They're talking about building an entire village here and living together."

Wist had a huge smile on her face as she listened. "You should come with me into the forest. I have the perfect person for you to meet. Really one of a kind, just like you."

The people got to work building a village where all of them could live together. Everyone had something to offer. Sherry made sure everyone was listened to and encouraged them when the work was hard. Curio and Persephone planned where everything should be built, and Brim brought stone from deep underground so Curio didn't have to make it all.

Kiria the sky queen gave the orders with kindness, keeping everyone on task. Molly grew beautiful flowers where she could and became surprisingly good friends with the goblins, who helped in any way they could. They splashed colorful paint on the buildings. They arranged sparkling stones in strange places. They didn't stop until the village was welcoming to all, even their quiet friend Pinn. Pinn spent her time away from the noise, but when she returned, she carried a sign. It was painted sky blue, with red and yellow and purple flowers, and a message in the middle: "Welcome to Dewdrop Hill." They put it next to the road that led into the village.

Wist went on to many other great adventures, but her first one was introducing Molly to Beauty, the great tree in the forest.

No one is exactly alike, and everyone wants something different. It can be so much easier to spend your life around people who are just like you, or even all by yourself. But when everyone works together and no one is forgotten, everyone is living in a better place.

Leave Your Feedback on Amazon

Please think about leaving some feedback via a review on Amazon. It may only take a moment, but it really does mean the world for small authors like myself :)

Even if you did not enjoy this title, please let me know the reason(s) in your review so that I may improve this title and serve you better.

From the Author

As a retired school teacher, my mission with this series is to create premium inspirational content for children that will help them be strong in the body, mind, and spirit via important life lessons and motivational messages.

Without you, however, this would not be possible, so I sincerely thank you for your purchase and for supporting my life's mission.

Made in United States
North Haven, CT
02 September 2023

41056750R00065